Earth is a planet traveling through space. It circles around the Sun once every year. If you were looking at Earth from the Moon, you would see a blue, brown, and green planet covered with wisps of white. If you watched long enough, you would see the planet spinning like a slow-motion top. It takes exactly 24 hours for Earth to make one complete turn.

There are eight other planets circling the Sun, but only Earth has air you can breathe, water you can swim in, and trees you can climb. It is the only planet where you can live without a space suit.

Earth's atmosphere also transports water to every part of the planet. When a puddle evaporates or your swimsuit dries, the water doesn't just disappear. The liquid water changes into a gas called *water vapor*. Water vapor rises into the air and is blown about by the wind. If conditions are right, water vapor condenses in small drops of water, and forms a cloud.

From space, astronauts can look through the clouds and see Earth's oceans. The great oceans of Earth—the Atlantic, Pacific, Indian, and Arctic—are really one enormous sea. They cover about 70 percent of the planet. Some parts of the ocean are over six miles deep. Humans have walked on the Moon, but we have yet to explore the furthest depths of the sea.

Earth's oceans are filled with salt water. A different type of water can be found in the rivers, lakes, and ponds that dot the continents. These smaller bodies of water contain fresh water.

There is a constant movement of water between the oceans and the land. Water evaporates from the ocean, forms clouds, and falls as rain or snow upon the continents. The water then drains into rivers and eventually flows back to the ocean. Some rivers, like the Amazon River in South America, are so wide in places that you cannot see across them to the other side.

As water flows to the sea, it slowly changes the land. Most rivers, even the

cover some of Earth's highest mountains. The Himalayan Mountains, the world's tallest, are more than five miles high. Hundreds of glaciers carve the mountains' upper slopes. Where the glaciers have melted, enormous U-shaped valleys reveal the power of the flowing ice.

The land we live on is always changing. Glaciers carve deep valleys, and rivers wear canyons and channels. Even the mountains that tower above the horizon do not stay the same. They formed long ago, as the Earth's surface slowly bulged and buckled. As time passes, the mountains are worn away by rain, wind, and snow. These dramatic changes happen slowly, over millions of years.

The Hawaiian islands were formed by a chain of volcanoes.

Earth is a unique planet. The air, the water, and even the land are in constant motion. Earth is also the only planet known to support life. Nearly every square foot of our planet's surface contains some form of living organism. Life exists even in the deepest parts of the sea and on the coldest Arctic ice.

The first creatures on Earth lived in the sea. Today the oceans are home to life of every sort, from tiny, single-celled plankton to whales, the largest creatures on Earth. Every creature on Earth needs water to live, and there is plenty of water in the sea.

All the organisms on Earth depend on each other in intricate ways. Plants produce oxygen from rocks, water, carbon dioxide, and sunlight. Animals breathe the oxygen, exhale carbon dioxide, and devour the plants. Plant-eating animals, in turn, are preyed upon by meat eaters. The remains of dead animals end up as fertilizer for plants.

Much like the wind and rain, living organisms shape our planet in many ways. Sea creatures called *coral* grow in enormous colonies that sometimes become large enough to form islands. On prairies and savannas, grasses prevent the wind from blowing away topsoil. In a similar manner, trees and bushes keep rain from washing away the land. Without life, Earth would be nothing but rock and water.

Some of the biggest changes on Earth have been caused by human beings. We have built great cities, dammed rivers to create lakes, and turned deserts into rich cropland. We have shaped Earth to make it easier for us to live.

Unfortunately, many of our actions are damaging the planet. Factories pollute the air, garbage dumps spoil the land, and oil spills contaminate the sea. To make room for more cropland, people are burning tropical rain forests. We are even destroying the ozone that protects us from the sun's ultraviolet radiation.

Of all the creatures on Earth, only humans have the power to save—or to destroy—our planet. We are learning that everything we do to the air, to the land, and to the water affects our entire world.

The planet Earth is our home. It is also home to trillions of other living things. Scientists think that in 5 billion years the Sun will expand, making Earth uninhabitable. Until then, if we make the right choices, Earth will be a pleasant place to live.